YOUR KNOWLEDGE HAS VALUE

Bibliographic information published by the German National Library:

The German National Library lists this publication in the National Bibliography; detailed bibliographic data are available on the Internet at http://dnb.dnb.de .

Imprint:

Copyright © 2012 GRIN Verlag, Open Publishing GmbH
Print and binding: Books on Demand GmbH, Norderstedt Germany
ISBN: 9783668372603

This book at GRIN:

http://www.grin.com/en/e-book/350712/the-creation-of-a-precedence-in-humani-tarian-affairs-through-the-blend

Anna Scheithauer

The Creation of a Precedence in Humanitarian Affairs through the Blend of International Legalization and World Politics

Multilateral Humanitarian Intervention: from an Exception to the Norm

GRIN Publishing

GRIN - Your knowledge has value

Since its foundation in 1998, GRIN has specialized in publishing academic texts by students, college teachers and other academics as e-book and printed book. The website www.grin.com is an ideal platform for presenting term papers, final papers, scientific essays, dissertations and specialist books.

Visit us on the internet:

http://www.grin.com/

http://www.facebook.com/grincom

http://www.twitter.com/grin_com

University of Illinois at Urbana-Champaign

PS 300: Special Topics – Politics in International Treaties

Spring 2012

The Creation of a Precedence in Humanitarian Affairs through the Blend of International Legalization and World Politics

Multilateral Humanitarian Intervention: from an Exception to the Norm

Anna Scheithauer

1

Table of Contents

Introduction

The research paper sets out to explore the motivations behind Security Council Resolution (SCR) 688 on the internal civilian situation in Iraq after the Gulf War in 1991 embodying the jump-start for the implementation of the today well-known concept of multilateral humanitarian interventions with the international community intervening in a states' domestic affaires on humanitarian grounds. Thereby, the puzzle surrounding the document evolves around the question of its content's legitimacy with view to international law and political implications, figuring a rather grey area which, however, had a tremendous impact on future actions, commitments and reasonings applied by the international community. Thus, the central questions the paper addresses in this regard relate to the debate on the impact of norms as a lock-in mechanism in international treaty law reflecting on how and why at exactly this point in time a new principle respectively doctrine was born.

For this purpose the examination of the intertwining of systemic changes in the world system with the international community's moral convictions, political inferences and the forms of legalization chosen will shed a light on the origination, the content and impacts of SCR 688 supporting the creation of a new world order. Thereby, special emphasis will on the political reasonings in the Security Council of the United Nations as well as on the three dimensions of legalization, namely, precision, obligation and delegation. In this respect, the interpretive function of international law (IL) together with a change in perception of human rights by the international community triggering an alteration of international norms will be clearly addressed. Hence, the findings will draw attention to how SCR 688 served as a precedence for all multilateral humanitarian interventions leading to a change in the conception of state sovereignty and the raise of a moral conviction of a "Responsibility to Protect" (R2P) by the international community producing long-term effects in international relations.

Altogether, the research paper will shed light on the complexity of issues at hand leading to a change in conceptual thinking and with it to the ignition of a revolutionary spark for an exception to the rules to becoming a normative principle. At the same time, it will show that generalizations within the realm of normative changes cannot be inferred from this unique example drawing rather to the aspect of a "ripe moment" in world affaires, with the exception of the blend of world politics and international legalization which seems a plausible set of factors underlying any transformative undertakings embodying the basis for the creation and progression of international law.

Starting out, some brief background information on the civilian situation in Iraq in 1991 as well as on UN Charter implications as to interference into a state's internal affaires in this respect shall draw attention to the intricacy of the situation the international community saw itself confronted with.

It was at the end of the Gulf War that the worst humanitarian crisis for especially the Kurdish people of Iraq was yet to come. Following George Bush's call for "the Iraqi military and the Iraqi people to take matters into their own hands and force Saddam Hussein, the dictator, to step aside" (Dodge 2009) As a consequence, Kurdish and Shi'a uprisings in the north and south of Iraq started on 1st and 3rd March 1991 with the government of Saddam Hussein counter-reacting with heavy gun fires and military attacks through among others artillery cannons and helicopters killing thousands of unarmed civilians. Moreover, the government regime set out to execute people even in homes and hospitals committing atrocities which spread fear and terror causing two million of Iraqis to flee to the mountains along the northern borders, the southern marshes and into Turkey and Iran exposed to harsh weather conditions lacking sufficient food and medial care. It was estimated by Greenpeace that due to the hardships refugees and IDPs had to endure during the exodus, daily death rates averaged about 1,000 from April to June 1991. (Human rRights Watch 1992)

This situation, as stated above, posed an immense challenge on the United Nations since as opposed to the Gulf War which embodied an armed conflict between two states allowing the United Nations to take actions in the name of individual and collective self-defense under Article 51 of Chapter VII of its Charter this humanitarian crisis was an internal matter of a sovereign state into which interference was strictly prohibited under UN Charter Article 2(4) stipulating "All Members shall refrain in their international relations from the threat or use of force against the territorial integrity or political independence of any state, or in any other manner inconsistent with the Purposes of the United Nations" and Article 2(7) pointing out that "Nothing contained in the present Charter shall authorize the United Nations to intervene in matters which are essentially within the domestic jurisdiction of any state [...]" (UN Charter 1945)

Considering the crisis and IL situation as just elaborated upon together with the fact that the international community had remained inactive in many similar situations in previous decades, it is interesting to explore why and how the UN "all of a sudden" was able got active on this matter.

A Changing World Order

First of all, when looking at the systemic level of analysis tremendous changes in the international environment can be noticed in and around the year 1991 with the end of the Cold War as the most decisive one creating a unipolar world with the United States emerging as the major global power. This brought about an ease in tensions and improvements of relations with Russia and an increase in multilateralism of all five permanent members on the Security Council (SC) which in previous decades had so often been dead-locked by either the United States or the Soviet Union exercising its veto power. (Malone 2008) Furthermore, a wave of democratization in the SC was to be noticed through the process of decolonization that had taken place from the 1960s onwards -a time where "authoritarian regimes have given way to more democratic forces and responsive Governments" (An Agenda for Peace 1992) - multiplying not only the number of UN member states in the General Assembly but also increasing the pool and regions the rotating non-permanent members were drawn from.

Also the decline in inter-state wars and the increase in intra-state armed conflicts taking on disastrous – often genocidal - dimensions facilitated by a soar in technological advancements and, thus, sophistication of weaponry, as the new emerging trend as to patterns of warfare at the onset of an ever more globalized and interconnected respectively interdependent time has to be mentioned creating a new challenge to deal with for the international community. (Siegel 2010) This is well reflected in the UN's Agenda for Peace which states that the global transition is marked by contradictory trends with regional associations of states deepening cooperation on the one had and new assertions of nationalism and sovereignty springing up on the other, with brutal ethnic, religious, social, cultural and linguistic strives threatening the cohesion of states. This, moreover, suggested an increase in the complexity of human security and with it in international security shedding light on the importance of states to a strong commitment to human rights. (An Agenda for Peace)

As a result, a revival of Wilsonian ideas could be noticed as "the revolution in communications has united the world in awareness, in aspiration and in greater solidarity against injustice" (An Agenda for Peace 1992) opening the international community's eyes that "the sovereignty, territorial integrity and independence of States [...] and the principle of self-determination for peoples, both of great value and importance, must not be permitted to work against each other in the period ahead" (An Agenda for Peace 1992) leading to a heated debate on questions of legality and legitimacy and, in turn, to the emergence of a more comprehensive approach to peace, justice, security, and development. (Malone 2008)

(Geo) Political Motivations

However, before elaborating on the ideological and moral dimension of the arguments brought forward in the SC as well as on how to combine the international community's new convictions with the existing legal framework, some insights into the (geo) political interests in the region of the permanent SC members and affected powers will give an account of the complexity of issues at hand.

Iraqi President Saddam Hussein had for long been a thorn in the eye of the international community which had carefully monitored his extreme human rights violations in Iraq's domestic sphere as well as his hostile relations with some of the country's neighbors. Although a number of armed conflicts had erupted in previous decades Iraq's invasion of Kuwait in 1990 finally triggered the UN to intervene with the US as the leading power, since – among others – oil interests were clearly at stake. This geopolitical aspect behind measures taken can be stressed with US President George Bush Sr. declaring "Our jobs, our way of life, our own freedom ... would all suffer if control of the world's great oil reserves fell into the hands of Saddam Hussein." (Global Policy Forum 2002) let alone Iraq's nuclear weapons program and the country's possession of biological and chemical weapons as had become evident during the Iran-Iraq war. (Global Policy Forum 2002)

The paragraph above, clearly shows the economic and security concerns for particularly the US and Great Britain, which had been Iraq's colonial power and also major trading partner in oil as had/has been France, the only one of the great powers that had still remained friendly relations with Saddam Hussein up until the happenings in 1991. (Astier 1998)

Negative economic impacts as well as political ones with view to the threat of a multi-fold increase in their own Kurdish minorities were also one of the main fears of Turkey and Iran who saw themselves faced to deal with an influx of refugees across their common border with Iraq. This caused Turkey to close its borders further aggravating the humanitarian crisis for the Iraqi Kurds, and to appeal in a letter together with Iran and France - it features a large Kurdish diasporic community with its political centre in Paris - to the United Nations to become active on this matter pointing to the effects for regional peace and security. (Yearbook of the United Nations 1991)

Moral Convictions & Legal Considerations

The UN seeing itself presented with this request by Turkey, Iran and France combined with the fact that due to its previous involvement in Iraq which had caused genocide-like "side effects" for Iraq's civilian population with the sanctions mechanisms put in place under SCR 660 to end the Gulf War leading to a humanitarian catastrophe in Iraq, (Tiler, Sadiq 2002) certainly triggered the motivation to "right a wrong" as well as to follow through on the Iraq case with the latter view predominantly expressed by the United Kingdom (Mills 1998) But in this regard, the literature also speculates that besides moral convictions Prime Minister John Major was also motivated by a need to appear domestically more decisive in his leadership skills. Also the fact that, Turkey being a NATO member and having supported coalition efforts against Iraq during the Gulf War, contributed to the pressure for the international community to come to aid. (Murphy, 1996)

Furthermore, there was this overall atmosphere that it would not be legitimate for the international community to close its eyes and to remain inactive on the Kurdish crisis with the whole world watching as the CNN effect created awareness about the extremity of the situation which no longer made possible to ignore gross violations of human rights committed within a sovereign state "[...] generating domestic pressure to do something [...]" and, thus, turning them into an international concern. (Mills 1998)

As a consequence a heated debate on the internal situation of Iraq erupted in the SC under increasing time pressure to act with arguments put forward clearly divided among two fractions with the one side viewing any multilateral intervention into a states' domestic sphere as a violation of IL and the other calling for an exception to alleviate the suffering of Iraq's civilian population. Thus, an initial draft resolution was put together which was later adopted as SCR 688 under Chapter VI of the UN Charter but featuring strong mandatory language by 10 votes in favor (Austria, Belgium, Côte d'Ivoire, Ecuador, France, Romania, USSR, United Kingdom, United States, Zaire), 3 against (Cuba, Yemen, Zimbabwe) and 2, including one permanent member, abstaining (China and India). Now, let's explore the arguments around and about the resolution which in the end created such a precedence in IL. (Malanczuk 1991)

As already mentioned, Turkey, France and Iran stressed the transboundary impact of the internal situation posing not only a threat to regional but also international peace and security while the permanent representative of Iraq to the UN reminded about the "[...] sovereignty, territorial integrity and political independence of Iraq and of all states in the area". (Koshy 1996, 2760) But interestingly enough, although pressing for the international community to act on the

7

civilian crisis in Iraq, Turkey prolonged SC procedures as it was keen to avoid any recognition of a Kurdish identity in a possible resolution due to future political implications this might bring about objecting to the mentioning of the Kurds as a group in the draft resolution. (Koshy 1996)

Nevertheless, the former view was clearly supported by the US, Great Britain and Russia arguing that the Iraqi situation was creating a destabilizing situation in the area and posed the threat of a new international conflict. The interesting aspect to notice here is that Russia aligned itself with the Western countries. The literature states that the reasons for it can be seen in Russia's increasing dependence on the US for economic assistance as well as the fact that it had already lost its leverage in international affairs. (Koshy 1996)

On the other hand, the latter argument received backing by Yemen, Zimbabwe and Cuba with the latter adding to the discussion that questions of humanitarian nature do not fall under the competences of the SC but to the General Assembly (GA), and therefore the proper procedure would be to convene the GA. Also India argued with UN Charter Article 2(7) as it was particularly concerned about a future shift in the international spotlight over to Kashmir. But since India had become a member of the SC only in January 1991 and it was not prepared to displease the US as important negotiations on economic issues in which the role of the US was crucial were about to come up, India preferred to abstain from the vote rather than to object. Finally, China as a permanent member of the SC also supported the traditionalist view as it, like India, had an "internal problem", namely Tibet. But as China had very rarely used its veto power in the previous decades and did not want to displease the US either, predominantly because of economic considerations, it also decided to abstain on the vote rather than to exercise its veto power. (Koshy 1996)

Counteracting on Iraq's et al. objections, France embodying the birth place of universalist thought during the Age of Enlightenment, pointed to the universal character of human rights stating that "violations of human rights such as those now being observed become a matter of international interest,when they take on such proportions that they assume the dimension of a crime against humanity" (Koshy 1996, 2761) In fact, long before the Iraqi case, French non-governmental organizations had advocated for a right to take emergency humanitarian action in a state without the consent of the government and saw this as a new chance to re-advocate their universalist stance in world politics. (Murphy 1996) Germany and Austria, aware of their own historical record, backed up the French representative with Germany proclaiming that "[...] Iraqi government actions harbor the danger of genocide" (Koshy 1996, 2761) and Austria noting "From our own history, we know that peace was most threatened when human rights were abolished and minorities persecuted, and when democratic processes gave way to totalitarian practices." (Murphy 1996, 178) Also the UK supported this cosmopolitan view opining that sovereignty is not a veil that human rights abusers can hide behind. It stressed that, actually, state authorities are responsible of protecting the safety and lives of their citizens. Hence, this holds that extreme cases of human suffering would create a legitimate moral exception to the rule of non-intervention. (Bellamy 2004)

Altogether, it soon became clear that the majority of member countries in the SC was convinced about the necessity to intervene on humanitarian grounds into Iraqi affaires without any of the permanent members casting a possible veto. But now that it is largely clarified why the international community at exactly this point in time was ready to multilaterally intervene into the domestic affaires of a state, the question still remains how this change in norms was translated into a legal doctrine.

Legalization: New Meanings to Old Contexts

The legalization of the intervention was brought about by the reinterpretation of existing law featuring arguments such as the UK's pointing out that UN Charter Article 2(7) would "[...] not apply to matters which under, the charter, are not essentially domestic and we have often seen human rights - for example in South Africa - defined in that category". (Koshy 1996, 2761) In this respect, it was argued that the equal importance of human rights when compared and contrasted with the notion of state sovereignty is well reflected in the UN Charter, namely, in Article 1(3) stating that one of the purposes of the United Nations is the achievement of international cooperation in furthering respect for human rights as well as Article 55 reaffirming that the UN shall promote comprehensive support and observance of fundamental human rights. (Gallant 1992) With it came the reinterpretation of UN Charter Article 39 so that threats to international peace and security, as was stressed by Turkey, France, etc. to clearly be the case in the Iraq crisis, could no longer be considered as confined to military acts of aggression allowing the international community to legally and legitimately carry out a humanitarian intervention. (Duke 1994) From then onwards, the time of absolute and exclusive state sovereignty was over stressing the state's obligation of good internal governance and leading to a "Responsibility to Protect" of the international community should it fail to do so. (Agenda for Peace 1992)

Thus, a legal and legitimate framework for SCR 688 was established. However, when examining the three functions of legalization grey areas can be detected in the resolution. As to obligation it can be noticed that SCR 688 was certainly legal as it featured a SC mandate and was, as we've just learned above, in compliance with IL. However, it is rather low as it is seen to embody a mere soft law document under Chapter VI of the UN Charter requiring the consent of the Iraqi government (Murphy 1996) – this was never obtained as stipulated in the Memorandum of Understanding with Iraq (Fenton 2004) – outlawing any enforcement mechanisms. Nevertheless, Article 5 of the resolution causes for some confusion as it features strong mandatory language allowing for measures which would actually require a Chapter VII mandate. (Murphy 1996) Thus, with view to the delegation function, the resolution can be suggested to be rated as "fair" due to, on the one hand, the firmness of appeals and requests, and on the other, the absence of the consent by Iraq and the lack of authorization for clear enforcement action. Furthermore, the unclarity in obligation is well reflected in the precision function of legalization which can be rated "very low" as SCR 688 is quite vague lacking any concrete content with view to clear measures to be taken. (SCR 688 1991)

Nevertheless, despite all the ambiguities the response of the UN based on SCR 688 might have immediately brought about a new principle was born and a thousands of lives could have been saved. In this respect it is to notice that SCR 688 was produced under immense time pressure and it is not to forget that with this precedence set the international community had no prior similar experiences it would have been able to rely on so that it seems rather natural that mistakes were made during the first-time ever multilateral humanitarian intervention. (Gallant 1992) However, the UN has certainly learned from the past gradually building up a comprehensive system around and about humanitarian interventions in the last decades. A most recent example is SRC 1973 of 2011 authorizing a humanitarian intervention in Libya, this time with the right mandate for the actions to be taken, namely, under Chapter VII of the UN Charter embodying a peace enforcement action. (SCR 1973 2011)

Conclusion

As we have come to see, it was indeed the blend of world politics and legalization at a time of systemic change that a precedence in humanitarian affaires was created with what was initially seen an exception to the rules becoming the norm with a mere and flawed soft law document serving as the lock-in mechanism for this new principle in place. But what the complexity of the debate has also shown is that no generalization can be inferred from this case but that rather depending on the set of circumstances and actors each change in norms relies on a "ripe moment" carrying enough momentum to make it, through whatever mechanism, an everlasting one!

Bibliography

Astier, Henri. 1998 "Iraq: the French connection", Decision Makers and Diplomacy, BBC News, 23 February

Bellamy, Alex J. 2004. "Ethics and Intervention: The 'Humanitarian Exception' and the Problem of Abuse in the Case of Iraq", Journal of Peace Research, Vol. 41, No. 2 (March): pp. 131- 147, Published by: Sage Publications, Ltd.

Boutrous-Ghali, Boutrous. 1992. "An Agenda for Peace - Preventive Diplomacy, Peacemaking and Peace-keeping", report of the Secretary-General pursuant to the statement adopted by the Summit Meeting of the Security Council on 31 January 1992

Dodge, Toby. 2009. "What accounts for the evolution of International Policy towards Iraq 1990-2003?", The Iraq Inquiry, Queen Mary University of London (November)

Duke, Simon. 1994. "The State and Human Rights: Sovereignty Versus Humanitarian Intervention", David Davies Memorial Institute for International Studies, International Relations, SAGE Publications, pp. 25-48

Fenton, Neil. 2004. "Northern Iraq 1991" in Understanding the UN Security Council: Coercion or Consent?", Ashgate Publishing Limited, Hampshire/England, pp. 37-63

Gallant, Judy A. 1992. "Conclusion" in "Humanitarian Intervention and Security Council Resolution 688: A Reappraisal in Light of a Changing World Order" American University International Law Review, Volume 7, Issue 4, Article 4, pp. 881-920

Global Policy Forum (GPF). "Chapter 4 - Causes of Human Suffering: 4.1. Iran-Iraq War and the Gulf War" ed. GPF, "Iraq Sanctions: Humanitarian Implications and Options for the Future" 6 August 2002, http://www.globalpolicy.org/component/content/article/170/41947.html#4

Human Rights Watch (HRW). "Chapter Two: The March 1991 Uprisings: Introduction" ed. HRW "Endless Torment: The 1991 Uprising in Iraq And Its Aftermath" http://www.hrw.org/legacy/reports/1992/Iraq926.htm , United States of America, June 1992

Koshy, Ninan. 1996. "The United Nations, the US and Northern Iraq", Economic and Political Weekly, Vol. 31, No. 40 (5 October): pp. 2760-2765, Published by: Economic and Political

Malanczuk, Peter. 1991. "III. The Legality of the Allied Intervention" ed. Malanczuk, Peter. The
      Kurdish Crisis and Allied Intervention in the Aftermath of the Second Gulf War", pp. 123-
      130

Malone, David. 2008. "The International Struggle over Iraq: Politics in the UN Security Council,
      1980-2005 ", The American Journal of International Law, Vol. 102, No. 3 (July): pp. 687-
      691

Mills, Kurt. "United Nations intervention in refugee crises after the Cold War", The American
      University, Cairo/Egypt, International Politics 35.4, 1998, p. 394

Murphy, Sean D. 1996. "Incidents of Intervention after the Cold War: B Northern Iraq (1991) and
      Southern Iraq (1992)" ed. Murphy, Sean D. "Humanitarian Intervention: The United Nations
      in an Evolving World Order", University of Pennsylvania Press, pp. 165-198

Siegel, Kelly. 2010. "UN Intervention in Civil War and Post-Conflict Economic Recovery",
      Undergraduate Thesis, NYU 2010

Tiller, Sharon/Sadiq, Sheraz. 2002. "Iraq- Truth and Lies in Baghdad. The Debate over U.N.
      Sanctions", Frontline World, http://www.pbs.org/frontlineworld/stories/iraq/sanctions.html ,
      November 2002

United Nations. 1945. "Chapter I: Purposes and Principles" and "Chapter VII: Action with Respect
      to Threats to the Peace, Breaches of the Peace and Acts of Aggression" ed. United Nations
      "Charter of the United Nations", 26 June 1945

United Nations. 1991. "Kurdish and other Displaced Populations: Security Council Actions" ed.
      United Nations "Yearbook of the United Nations", Martinus Nijhoff Publishers, Dordrecht/the
      Netherlands, pp. 204-205

UN Security Council. 1991. "Resolution 688 (1991) - Adopted by the Security Council at its 2982nd
      meeting", 5 April 1991, http://www.casi.org.uk/info/undocs/gopher/s91/5
UN Security Council. 1991 "Resolution 1973 (2011) – Adopted by the Security Council at its 6498th
      meeting, 17 March 2011,
      http://daccess-ddsny.un.org/doc/UNDOC/GEN/N11/268/39/PDF/N1126839.pdfOpenElement

YOUR KNOWLEDGE HAS VALUE

- We will publish your bachelor's and master's thesis, essays and papers

- Your own eBook and book - sold worldwide in all relevant shops

- Earn money with each sale

Upload your text at www.GRIN.com
and publish for free